# A Note to Parents and Teachers

DK READERS is a compelling reading programme for children. The programme is designed in conjunction with leading literacy experts, including Cliff Moon M.Ed., who has spent many years as a teacher and teacher educator specializing in reading. Cliff Moon has written more than 160 books for children and teachers. He is series editor to Collins Big Cat.

Beautiful illustrations and superb full-colour photographs combine with engaging, easy-to-read stories to offer a fresh approach to each subject in the series. Each DK READER is guaranteed to capture a child's interest while developing his or her reading skills, general knowledge, and love of reading.

The five levels of DK READERS are aimed at different reading abilities, enabling you to choose the books that are exactly right for your child:

**Pre-level 1:** Learning to read
**Level 1:** Beginning to read
**Level 2:** Beginning to read alone
**Level 3:** Reading alone
**Level 4:** Proficient readers

The "normal" age at which a child begins to read can be anywhere from three to eight years old. Adult participation through the lower levels is very helpful for providing encouragement, discussing storylines and sounding out unfamiliar words.

No matter which level you select, you can be sure that you are helping your child learn to read, then read to learn!

D0332284

**DK**

LONDON, NEW YORK, MUNICH,
MELBOURNE, AND DELHI

**Series Editor** Deborah Lock
**Designer** Vikas Sachdeva
**Project Designer** Akanksha Gupta
**Art Director** Martin Wilson
**Production Editor** Sarah Isle
**Jacket Designer** Natalie Godwin

**Reading Consultant**
Cliff Moon, M.Ed.

First published in Great Britain by
Dorling Kindersley Limited
80 Strand, London WC2R 0RL

Copyright © 2012 Dorling Kindersley Limited
A Penguin Company

10 9 8 7 6 5 4 3 2 1
001-184582-June 2012

A CIP catalogue record for this book
is available from the British Library

ISBN: 978-1-40938-679-7

Colour reproduction by Colourscan, Singapore
Printed and bound in China by L.Rex Printing Co., Ltd.

The publisher would like to thank the following for their kind permission to
reproduce their photographs:
(Key: a-above; b-below/bottom; c-centre; f-far; l-left; r-right; t-top)
3 Getty Images: Asia Images. 4 Corbis: Peter Burian (c); Thomas Marent /
Visuals Unlimited (tl). Getty Images: Art Wolfe / Stone (b). 5 Corbis: DLILLC
(tr); Visuals Unlimited (c). 6-7 Getty Images: Asia Images. 6 Photolibrary:
Jurgen & Christine Sohns / FLPA (br). 7 Corbis: Thomas Marent, / Visuals
Unlimited (t). Getty Images: Daniel Berehulak / Staff / Getty Images News
(br). Photolibrary: Stockbrokerxtra Images (bc). 8 Corbis: Thomas Marent /
Visuals Unlimited (br). 9 Corbis: Thomas Marent / Visuals Unlimited (br).
Getty Images: Luciano Candisani / Minden Pictures (c). Photolibrary: Terry
Whittaker./ FLPA (bc). 10 Dreamstime.com: Lasse Kristensen (c). Getty
Images: Creative Crop / Digital Vision (cr); Ultra.F / Digital Vision (cb). 11
Getty Images: Rubberball / Erik Isakson. Photolibrary: Juniors Bildarchiv
(bc). 12-13 Photolibrary: Juniors Bildarchiv. 13 Getty Images: Pete Mcbride /
National Geographic (bl). Photolibrary: Juergen and Christine Sohns (crb). 14
Getty Images: Gerry Ellis / Minden Pictures (t). 15 Corbis: Herbert Kehrer (br).
Getty Images: Ingo Arndt / Minden Pictures. 15 Corbis: Herbert Kehrer (br).
16-17 Getty Images: Piotr Naskrecki / Minden Pictures. 16 Getty Images: SA
Team / Foto Natura / Minden Pictures (bl); Kevin Schafer / Minden Pictures
(br). 17 Getty Images: Stan Osolinski / Oxford Scientific (br). Photolibrary:
Juniors Bildarchiv (bl). 18 Getty Images: Reinhard Dirscherl / WaterFrame (bl).
18-19 Photolibrary: Luiz C Marigo. 19 Getty Images: Reinhard Dirscherl /
WaterFrame (bc); Claus Meyer / Minden Pictures (bl). 20 Science Photo
Library: Chris Hellier (clb). 20-21 Alamy Images: Chris Hellier. 21 Getty
Images: Christian Kober / Robert Harding World Imagery (bc); Thomas
Marent / Minden Pictures (br). Photolibrary: Nick Garbutt (bl). 22 Getty
Images: Keren Su / Photodisc (t); Tier Und Naturfotografie J & C Sohns / The
Image Bank (bl). 23 Getty Images: Ben Cranke / The Image Bank; Lori Epstein
/ National Geographic (br). 24 Corbis: Peter Burian (c). Getty Images: Brooke
Whatnall / National Geographic (bl). 25 Corbis: Anup Shah (bl). Getty
Images: Fuse (br); Copyright Tony Franco / Flickr. 26-27 Getty Images: Visuals
Unlimited, Inc. / John Abbott. 26 Photolibrary: Michel & Christine
Denis-Huot (t). 27 Corbis: DLILLC (br). Getty Images: Steve Allen /
Photodisc (bc); Ben Cranke / The Image Bank (bl). 28-29 Getty Images: Sune
Wendelboe / Lonely Planet Images. 28 Corbis: Martin Harvey (bl). 29 Corbis:
Darrell Gulin (bl). Photolibrary: Christian Heinrich (bc); Keith Levit (br). 30
Dreamstime.com: Robert Wisdom (bl). Getty Images: Fotosearch. 31 Corbis:
Herbert Kehrer (cb). Photolibrary: Berndt Fischer (t); National Geographic
Society (br). 32 Corbis: Tim Davis (cb); DLILLC (ca); Oliver Lassen (b).
Dreamstime.com: Michael Lynch (t).
Jacket images: Front: naturepl.com: Nick Garbutt

All other images © Dorling Kindersley
For further information see: www.dkimages.com

Discover more at
**www.dk.com**

# Contents

**DK** READERS

LEARNING
pre-level
1
TO READ

# Monkeys

A Dorling Kindersley Book

Smile, please!
Come and meet
the monkeys
of the world.

A pygmy marmoset can fit in your hand. It's the smallest monkey.

marmosets

claw

tail

Golden lion tamarins climb up tree trunks and run along branches.

tamarins

golden
fur

branch

Capuchin monkeys
eat fruit, insects,
crabs and eggs.

fruit

crab

insects

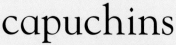
capuchins

A squirrel monkey
jumps from tree to tree.
Its baby hangs on tight.

squirrel monkeys

baby

hand

13

arm

A spider monkey
uses its tail to hang
from a tree.

spider monkeys

_tail

Howler monkeys
call to each other.
They are the loudest
animals on land.

howlers

ear

mouth

fur

eye

night monkeys

Night monkeys have
large brown eyes
to see in the dark.

# Proboscis monkeys have big noses and bellies.

nose

proboscis monkeys

belly

snow

Japanese macaques
keep warm in
the hot springs.

macaques

# hot
# spring

A large mandrill shows its teeth to make friends or scare enemies.

nose

**mandrills**

teeth

feet

vervet monkeys

Vervet monkeys
help each other
to keep clean.

____fur

Troops of baboons travel and live together.

**baboons**

Which monkeys

The monkeys rest
after being so busy.
Shh!

did you like best?

# Glossary

**Claw**
a sharp nail on
the end of an animal's
hands or toes

**Fur**
a thick coat of soft
hair that covers
an animal's skin

**Tail**
a long, movable
body part joined to
an animal's bottom

**Teeth**
used for biting and
chewing food

**Troop**
a group of monkeys,
also called a tribe